W9-DDA-098

J981 S

Brazil /

3338 003711894

J981
S

BRAZIL

SOUTH AMERICA
TODAY

BRAZIL

Charles J. Shields

Mason Crest Publishers
Philadelphia

Produced by OTTN Publishing, Stockton, N.J.

Mason Crest Publishers
370 Reed Road
Broomall, PA 19008
www.masoncrest.com

First printing

1 3 5 7 9 8 6 4 2

Library of Congress Cataloging-in-Publication Data

Shields, Charles J., 1951-
    Brazil / Charles J. Shields.
        p. cm. — (South America today)
    Includes index.
    ISBN 978-1-4222-0633-1 (hardcover) — ISBN 978-1-4222-0700-0 (pbk.)
    1. Brazil—Juvenile literature. [1. Brazil.] I. Title.
    F2508.5.S53 2008
    981—dc22
                                            2008032308

SOUTH AMERICA
TODAY

Argentina		Paraguay
Bolivia	**South America:**	Peru
Brazil	Facts & Figures	Suriname
Chile	Ecuador	Uruguay
Colombia	Guyana	Venezuela

Table of Contents

Discovering South America

James D. Henderson

South America is a cornucopia of natural resources, a treasure house of ecological variety. It is also a continent of striking human diversity and geographic extremes. Yet in spite of that, most South Americans share a set of cultural similarities. Most of the continent's inhabitants are properly termed "Latin" Americans. This means that they speak a Romance language (one closely related to Latin), particularly Spanish or Portuguese. It means, too, that most practice Roman Catholicism and share the Mediterranean cultural patterns brought by the Spanish and Portuguese who settled the continent over five centuries ago.

Still, it is never hard to spot departures from these cultural norms. Bolivia, Peru, and Ecuador, for example, have significant Indian populations who speak their own languages and follow their own customs. In Paraguay the main Indian language, Guaraní, is accepted as official along with Spanish. Nor are all South Americans Catholics. Today Protestantism is making steady gains, while in Brazil many citizens practice African religions right along with Catholicism and Protestantism.

South America is a lightly populated continent, having just 6 percent of the world's people. It is also the world's most tropical continent, for a larger percentage of its land falls between the tropics of Cancer and Capricorn than is the case with any other continent. The world's driest desert is there, the Atacama in northern Chile, where no one has ever seen a drop of rain fall. And the world's wettest place is there too, the Chocó region of Colombia, along that country's border with Panama. There it rains almost every day. South America also has some of the world's highest mountains, the Andes,

Rio de Janeiro, Brazil's second-largest city, is popular for its beautiful beaches.

and its greatest river, the Amazon.

So welcome to South America! Through this colorfully illustrated series of books you will travel through 12 countries, from giant Brazil to small Suriname. On your way you will learn about the geography, the history, the economy, and the people of each one. Geared to the needs of teachers and students, each volume contains book and web sources for further study, a chronology, project and report ideas, and even recipes of tasty and easy-to-prepare dishes popular in the countries studied. Each volume describes the country's national holidays and the cities and towns where they are held. And each book is indexed.

You are embarking on a voyage of discovery that will take you to lands not so far away, but as interesting and exotic as any in the world.

(Opposite) Iguaçu (or Iguazú) Falls is located at the point where Argentina, Brazil, and Paraguay meet. The breathtaking falls stretch for more than 2 miles (3.2 km), with drops of more than 260 feet (80 meters). (Right) Sugar Loaf Mountain, shown at sunset, towers over the entrance to Guanabara Bay near Rio de Janeiro.

1 Giant of South America

BRAZIL IS THE largest of the Latin American countries, and the fifth-largest country in the world after Russia, Canada, China, and the United States. Covering almost half of South America, it spans four time zones and borders every country on the continent except Chile and Ecuador. The equator passes through the north of the country near Macapá. The tropic of Capricorn passes through the south of the country near São Paulo. The Atlantic Ocean stretches across the eastern side of the country, giving it a coastline of 4,578 miles (7,367 kilometers).

Lowlands and Highlands

Two main features characterize the landscape of Brazil: the densely forested lowlands of the Amazon Basin in the north, and the generally open uplands of the Brazilian Highlands to the south. The Amazon River, with its surrounding lowland basin of 1,544,400 square miles (3,998,451 sq km), forms the largest rain forest in the world. In the south and southeast, the Brazilian Highlands—an eroded *plateau* dotted with irregular mountains and crossed by river valleys—forms the major feature of the landscape. A network of mountains runs from the south through the northeast, dividing the interior of Brazil from the Atlantic Ocean.

The most extensive lowland is the Amazon Basin. Most of the area is gently rolling terrain, rarely rising more than 490 feet (149 meters) above sea level. Seasonal flooding occurs along the Amazon River through stretches of flat, swampy land called *varzeas*. A second major lowland is the Pantanal in the western Mato Grosso area near the border with Bolivia and Paraguay. Seasonal flooding occurs in this region along the headwaters of the Paraná and Paraguay river system. The third lowland area is the *coastal plain*. In northeastern Brazil it may be up to 40 miles (64 km) wide, but in some places it is very narrow. Between Rio de Janeiro and Santos it disappears entirely. The coastal plain has been a major area of settlement and economic activity since colonial times. Twelve of the country's state capitals are located along it. The plain widens in the southern part of the state of Rio Grande do Sul and extends into Argentina.

Much of the rest of Brazil lies between 700 feet (214 meters) and 2,600 feet (793 meters) in elevation. The Brazilian Highlands, an enormous block of geologically ancient rocks, occupies most of the southern half of the country. The mountain ranges that run through parts of the highlands include the Serra da Mantiqueira, the Serra do Espinhaço, the Chapada Diamantina, and the

Serra do Mar. The Serra do Mar forms a sharp edge along the coast from Rio de Janeiro south for about 600 miles (966 km) into the state of Santa Catarina. Some cliffs stand 2,600 feet (793 meters) above the shore. Behind the Serra do Mar, an extensive plateau reaches through the state of São Paulo and into the southern states.

In the far north the Guiana Highlands cover only 2 percent of the country. These highlands form a major drainage divide, separating rivers that flow south into the Amazon Basin from rivers that empty into the Orinoco river system of Venezuela to the north. The highest point in Brazil—the 9,888-foot (3,014-meter) Pico da Neblina—is in the mountains of the Guiana Highlands.

Largest River System in the World

Brazil has a dense and complex system of rivers. The Amazon is the world's second-longest river, after the Nile in Egypt. Based on the amount of

A view of Rio de Janeiro, including Copacabana Beach. The coastal cities of Brazil enjoy warm temperatures all year.

water drained, however, the Amazon and its *tributaries* rank as the largest river system in the world.

Brazil's coastline varies considerably. In the north, at the equator, the mouth of the Amazon breaks up the coast with major river channels, lowlands, swamps of mangrove trees, and numerous islands. Farther south and east, the coast becomes smoother, with large areas of beaches and dunes. Dunes, mangroves, lagoons, and hills can be found south of Cape São Roque, near easternmost Brazil.

As the coastline curves gently westward south of the cities of Natal and Recife, lagoons, marshlands, sand spits, and sandy beaches can all be found. In the states of Espírito Santo, Rio de Janeiro, and São Paulo, and parts of the south, the mountains come close to the coast. At the foot of them, the coastal

A Brazilian farm worker sets a section of the rain forest ablaze to clear the land. The rain forest is one of Brazil's natural treasures; however, large segments of it continue to be destroyed, permanently damaging the environment.

plain is narrow or nonexistent. Only in the state of Rio Grande do Sul does the plain widen again. Portuguese settlers established their first communities along the coast, and most Brazilians still live within about 200 miles (322 km) of the coast.

Generally Mild Climate

Although 90 percent of the country lies in the tropical zone, most of the population lives in areas where altitude, sea winds, or cold fronts create moderate temperatures. P[...]h [...] São Paulo, Bras[í]lia, and Belo Horizonte have very mil[...] cities such as Rio de Janeiro, Recife, [...] and Pôrto Alegre, the cooler subtr[...] the United States and Europe. In su[...]o is hot and humid with temperature[...]mperatures usually hover around 77[...]ot as Rio in the summer, but tropica[...]. Northeast Brazil is the hottest part[...]en May and November, temperature[...]he Brazilian winter, which lasts from [...]. The coolest southern states enjoy average winter temperatures that range between 55°F (13°C) and 64°F (18°C).

The Amazon Basin is the rainiest part of Brazil. While this area is quite humid, temperatures are surprisingly moderate, averaging only 80°F (27°C). The heaviest rainfall in Brazil occurs around the mouth of the Amazon River,

Quick Facts: The Geography of Brazil

Location: eastern South America, bordering the Atlantic Ocean

Area: (slightly smaller than the United States)

total: 3,286,470 square miles (8,511,965 sq km)

land: 3,265,059 square miles (8,456,510 sq km)

water: 21,411 square miles (55,455 sq km)

Terrain: mostly flat to rolling lowlands in north; some plains, hills, mountains, and narrow coastal belt

Natural hazards: recurring droughts in northeast; floods and occasional frost in south

Borders: Argentina, 761 miles (1,225 km); Bolivia, 2,113 miles (3,400 km); Colombia, 1,021 miles (1,643 km); French Guiana, 418 miles (673 km); Guyana, 695 miles (1,118 km); Paraguay, 802 miles (1,291 km); Peru, 969 miles (1,559 km); Suriname, 371 miles (597 km); Uruguay, 612 miles (985 km); Venezuela, 1,367 miles (2,200 km)

Elevation extremes:

lowest point: Atlantic Ocean—0 feet

highest point: Pico da Neblina—9,888 feet (3,014 meters)

Climate: mostly tropical, but temperate in south

Source: CIA World Factbook 2001.

near the city of Belém, and also in upper Amazonia, where more than 78 inches (198 cm) of rain falls every year. Unlike the Amazon region, however, most of Brazil experiences moderate rainfall, usually between 39 inches (99 cm) and 59 inches (150 cm) a year. Most of this rain falls between December and April, while the winter months tend to be dry.

First in the World for Species

The richness and diversity of Brazil's *flora* and *fauna* are astounding. The country ranks first in the world for numbers of species of mammals, freshwater fish, and plants; second for amphibians; third for birds; and fifth for reptiles.

Of an estimated 750 mammal species in South America, 394 are found in Brazil. Larger mammals include pumas, jaguars, ocelots, rare bush dogs, and foxes. Peccaries, tapirs, anteaters, sloths, opossums, and armadillos are abundant. Deer are plentiful in the south, and monkeys of many species abound in the rain forests. The country has one of the world's most diverse populations of birds and amphibians, with 1,635 species of birds and 502 species of amphibians. Brazil's great variety of reptiles includes lizards, snakes, turtles, and alligators. The number of species of freshwater fish in Brazil is estimated at more than 1,500, of which more than 1,000 are found in the Amazon Basin. In addition, an enormous number of invertebrates (species that lack a spinal column) inhabit Brazil. The total is believed to exceed 100,000 species, of which 70,000 are insects.

The Amazon rain forest contains the largest single reserve of biological organisms—both animal and plant—in the world. No one really knows how many species there are in the Amazon, but scientists estimate the number could be as high as 5 million, amounting to 15 to 30 percent of all the species in the entire world.

Unfortunately, Brazil is also notorious for the destruction of its environment. All of the country's major ecosystems—not just the well-known Amazonia—are threatened. Major threats to Brazil's rich flora and fauna include the continued logging of rain forests, draining of wetlands in the northeast, poaching in the Pantanal region, and coastal pollution.

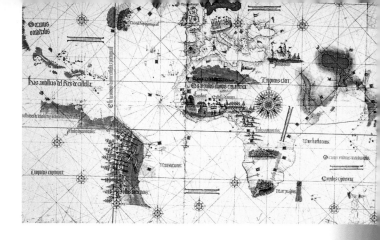

(Right) This section of a 1502 map of the world shows the coastline of Brazil, which had been "discovered" by the Portuguese navigator Pedro Álvares Cabral two years earlier. The Brazil area was already inhabited by millions of Native Americans; these Guarani men, holding traditional weapons, are among their descendants.

2 A Legacy of Inequality

BRAZIL'S HISTORY CAN be divided into two major parts: the colonial era (1500 to 1821) and the post-independence period (1822 to the present). Colonial Brazil became the first great plantation society in the Americas. Using slave labor, its large agricultural estates produced sugar and, later, coffee. After Brazil broke away from Portugal in the 1820s, members of the Portuguese royal family ruled the South American country as emperors until 1889. Since 1889, Brazil has been a *republic*.

For centuries, Brazil has been a land where Europeans, Amerindians (American Indians), and Africans intermingled, producing one of the most racially mixed societies in the world. But it is also a nation of deep and lasting social and economic gaps between its peoples.

17

Colonization and Slavery

Most of the hundreds of Amerindian tribes living in eastern South America before the arrival of Europeans were members of the Tupí-Guaraní cultures. They generally survived by hunting and gathering. Those who farmed mainly raised manioc, also known as cassava. These *indigenous* peoples had no metal tools; no written language; no horses, llamas, or donkeys; and no knowledge of the wheel. Best estimates place the native population of eastern South America in 1500 at somewhere between 1 and 6 million. Today there may be as few as 350,000, most of them in the remote jungles of the Brazilian interior.

In 1499 the Portuguese explorer Vasco da Gama arrived back in Lisbon, Portugal, having made the first successful voyage from western Europe around the southern tip of Africa to India—a center for the profitable trade in spices, pearls, and precious stones. The Portuguese quickly outfitted a second expedition, led by Pedro Álvares Cabral, a young nobleman. In 1500 Cabral set sail from Lisbon with 13 ships and a crew of 1,200.

Cabral followed a more westerly course than had Vasco da Gama, and, carried by wind and tide, his fleet landed on the coast of South America in what is today Brazil on April 22, 1500. Cabral named his discovery Terra da Vera Cruz ("Land of the True Cross") and claimed it for Portugal.

King João III of Portugal sent the first settlers to Brazil in 1531. Three years later, he divided the coast into 15 sections, placing them under the private ownership of friends of the crown.

The colonists soon discovered that the land and climate were ideal for growing sugarcane. Plantations required plentiful labor, though. Portuguese plantation owners tried a number of methods to force the indigenous people to work in the sugar fields, but none worked well. So the colony resorted to slavery. *Bandeirantes*, men from São Paulo usually born of Indian mothers and Portuguese fathers, hunted the Indians into the interior. By the mid-1600s, they had pursued their prey all the way to the peaks of the Peruvian Andes.

The embattled Indians found an ally in members of the Society of Jesus, or Jesuits. Priests from this Roman Catholic teaching and missionary order had arrived in Bahia in 1549 with Thome de Souza, Brazil's first governor. A group of Jesuits, led by Manoel da Nobrega and José de Anchieta, eventually created a system of *aldeias* (villages) to Christianize the Indians. By the 1560s and 1570s the Jesuits had gathered thousands of indigenous people in dozens of protected *aldeias*.

The colonists, now more than ever unable to find an adequate supply of forced labor, expanded the slave trade. The Portuguese had begun the Atlantic slave trade in the 1440s, carrying black Africans to Lisbon, Portugal's capital. Beginning in the mid-16th century, and particularly during the 17th century, African slaves replaced Indians on the plantations of Brazil.

Conditions on the plantations were typically quite harsh, and many slaves resisted their fate. *Quilombos*, communities of runaway slaves, were common throughout the colonial era. They ranged from small groups hidden in the forests to the great society of Palmares. Located in northeastern Brazil, Palmares—whose population may have reached as high as 20,000—survived for much of the 17th century. Its inhabitants repelled dozens of military incursions before finally succumbing to a Portuguese colonial force in 1694.

The arrival of thousands of African slaves transformed areas of Brazil into multiracial societies. Amerindian, European, and African peoples intermingled. For every white colonist in the early 17th century, there may have been as many as three African slaves. Some 80 percent of the people of the northeastern coast today are descendants of Africans.

In the 1690s, gold was discovered in Minas Gerais, creating the first gold rush in the Western Hemisphere. Brazilians and Portuguese flooded into the territory, and countless more slaves were brought from Africa to dig—and die—in the mines.

In 1763 the Portuguese king moved the colonial capital from Salvador to the booming city of Rio de Janeiro. Its location on the coast offered the perfect entry and exit point for colonists, slaves, gold, and goods. Wealth poured into Rio and from there into Portugal.

The link between Portugal and Brazil was broken when France invaded Portugal in 1807. Two days before the invasion, the Portuguese prince regent (a ruler governing in place of an absent or disabled monarch—in this case, the queen, who was insane) set sail for Brazil.

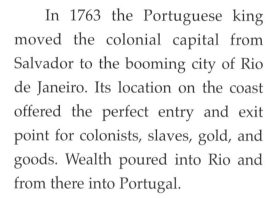

This 19th-century illustration shows slaves harvesting coffee on a Brazilian plantation. A white overseer sits in the shade while workers collect the beans. Thousands of Africans were brought to Brazil as slaves in the 16th and 17th centuries.

Soon after arriving, the prince regent (later to become King João VI) made Rio de Janeiro the capital of the United Kingdom of Portugal, Brazil, and the Algarve (a Moorish kingdom conquered in the 13th century and incorporated into Portugal).

On September 7, 1822, João VI's son Pedro proclaimed Brazil's independence from Portugal. He had himself crowned the nation's first emperor on October 22. The greatest challenge facing Emperor Pedro I was to keep his giant new nation from splintering into several countries, as had happened to the Spanish holdings in Central and South America.

Unfortunately, in the 1820s Pedro chose to fight Argentina over the southern border of Brazil. The struggle erupted into the Cisplatine War (1825–28). The war was unpopular with many Brazilians, especially after Brazil suffered a major military defeat at the hands of the Argentines in 1827. Pedro abdicated, or renounced, his Brazilian throne in 1831 and returned to Portugal.

By then Brazil had the largest slave population in the world, numbering several million. Although the slave trade was abolished in 1850, slavery remained legal in Brazil longer than in any other society in the Americas. The slave system finally began to crumble in the 1880s with the rise of an *abolitionist* movement and the increasing numbers of runaway slaves.

Coffee and Independence

The 1840s saw the beginning of large-scale coffee cultivation in Brazil. Like sugar, coffee was not native to the Americas. It had been carried there from the Mediterranean. Cultivation spread through the fertile valleys near Rio de Janeiro. During the 19th century, coffee replaced sugar as Brazil's major export and provided a tremendous amount of *revenue*, spurring Brazil's growth. At first the coffee plantations used slave labor, but with the abolition of slavery in 1888, thousands of European immigrants, mostly Italians, arrived to work on the coffee estates, called *fazendas*. About 100,000 European immigrants entered Brazil each year.

A small class of wealthy landowners dominated the country politically and economically, while the majority of Brazilians—mostly former slaves, their descendants, and the *mulatto* population—lived in poverty as agricultural workers. In 1889, a military *coup*, supported by the powerful coffee growers, toppled the Brazilian monarchy. A constituent assembly convened, and in June 1890 it completed the drafting of a constitution, which was adopted in February 1891. Similar to the Constitution of the United States, Brazil's constitution eliminated the monarchy and established a federal republic, officially called the United States of Brazil. For the next 40 years, Brazil was governed by a series of military and civilian presidents.

Unbalanced Progress

In 1929 the opposition Liberal Alliance was formed. The Liberal Alliance united many disaffected middle-class and urban groups, as well as most of the military. Its presidential candidate, Getúlio Vargas—whose election was stolen through fraud—was able to assume office thanks to a popular uprising.

Vargas went on to dominate Brazilian politics for the next 24 years. He succeeded in modernizing the country both politically and economically. Vargas's second presidential term was cut short by his suicide in 1954.

Vargas's successor and protegé, Juscelino Kubitschek, attempted to close the economic and social gaps between Brazil's rich and poor through fabulously expensive social programs. He built Brasília, the new capital, which was supposed to bring development to the vast interior of Brazil. But by the early 1960s, *inflation*—a continuing rise in prices—battered the economy and further eroded the standard of living of the nation's poor. For a time, it was feared that Brazil would turn to communism, inspired by Fidel Castro's victory in Cuba. That didn't happen, but in 1964 Brazil's fragile democracy was squashed by a military coup.

The military would rule Brazil for the next two decades. During that time, Brazil's economy improved dramatically. By the late 1960s the country was enjoying double-digit economic growth annually. Soon Brazil had become one of the economic powerhouses of the Western Hemisphere, helped by loans and investment from abroad. In 1985 the military handed power back to a civilian government, and Brazilians elected their president by popular vote for the first time

Getúlio Vargas was the most important Brazilian leader of the 20th century. He ruled Brazil for 18 years as both a dictator and a constitutionally elected president. While Vargas was in power, Brazil became more modern industrially and economically. His supporters nicknamed him "Father of the Poor" for his battles against big businesses and the reforms his administration instituted.

in more than 20 years.

Despite Brazil's remarkable success story, serious problems loomed. In the 1980s and into the 1990s, periodic bouts of inflation, accompanied by slow economic growth or complete stagnation, plagued the country. Brazil suddenly found itself struggling to pay its foreign debt, and investment dried up. Allegations of government incompetence and corruption were widespread.

In 1989 Fernando Collor de Mello ran for president promising to fight corruption and reduce inflation. He won by a narrow but secure majority. But by the end of 1992, Collor was himself indicted on charges of corruption. He was later cleared.

Vice President Itamar Franco became president in December 1992 upon Collor's resignation. The following year, inflation reached a staggering annual rate of 2,500 percent. To stabilize the economy and bring inflation under control, Franco's administration introduced a new currency, the *real* (pronounced *ray-AHL*). Eventually the measures paid off.

In November 1994, Fernando Cardoso, the economy minister widely credited with saving Brazil's economy, was elected president. Through the mid-1990s Cardoso presided over a Brazil having a growing economy, declining inflation, a stable currency, and record foreign investment. But 2 million jobs were eliminated and plans to help develop the poorer rural areas failed. In fact, a 1996 United Nations report showed that Brazil had the world's most unequal distribution of wealth.

Cardoso persuaded the Brazilian National Congress to change the constitution to allow him a second four-year term. He comfortably won the election in 1998. Following the election, the real was devalued, ushering in a period of economic belt-tightening. By 2000 the economy was growing again. But in mid-2002 another crisis loomed as the international financial markets, anxious about Brazil's huge public debt and the threat of renewed political instability, began to shun investment in Brazil's economy. The negative investor mood plunged the real to an all-time low.

A slumping economy usually signals difficult times for many people, just as a booming economy brings benefits to many. In Brazil, however, the poor have not only suffered the most in bad economic times but also frequently failed to see gains during good times. From the colonial era onward, Brazil has remained a society of deep and enduring economic and social inequalities. Poverty is widespread: more than 50 million Brazilians survive on less than one dollar per day. Gains in education, land reform, and welfare have been offset by a spotty health care system, urban overcrowding, rural landlessness, and environmental abuse. And, despite the beginnings of attempts to tackle the problem, corruption in Brazil remains a way of life.

Social problems were on the minds of Brazilian voters when, in October 2002, they elected Workers' Party candidate Luiz Inácio Lula da Silva to the presidency in the largest landslide in Brazilian history. A former labor union organizer, Lula—as he is popularly known—quickly announced his "solidarity with the Brazilians who have nothing to eat." He pledged to fight poverty, malnutrition and under-education through large-scale public-works projects, collectively called *Fome Zero* or "Zero Hunger." The programs seem to be making progress, and Lula vowed to expand them after his 2006 reelection. However, investors still wonder how Brazil can pay for Lula's programs while attempting to reduce its massive national debt.

Brazil has built South America's largest economy, but industrialization has led to environmental problems. (Opposite) the world's largest offshore oil rig—the size of a 40-story building—sinks off the coast of Macaé in March 2001, spilling some 400,000 gallons of crude and diesel oil into the ocean. (Right) Workers climb up the inside of a pit at the Sierra Pelada gold mine.

3 The Economy: Powerhouse Potential

BRAZIL BOASTS SOUTH America's largest economy, with a *gross domestic product*, or GDP, of $1.836 trillion in the year 2007, according to estimates by the United States CIA. (GDP is the total value of goods and services a country produces annually.)

From the late 1960s to the 1980s, many experts predicted that Brazil would become one of the world's leading economic powerhouses. It still may, though it will have to overcome a burdensome debt problem. By mid-2002, Brazil's public debt exceeded half of its GDP. What this means is that a huge amount of the wealth Brazil's economy creates must go to paying the interest on money the country has borrowed. In addition, social conditions rooted in the nation's early years as a plantation society continue to cause inequalities in

27

wealth and power. A small and wealthy *elite* still controls most of the land and resources while millions of Brazilians live in poverty, especially in rural areas.

Moving from a Single-Commodity Economy

Until the beginning of the 20th century, the Brazilian economy depended to a great extent on the production and export of a single commodity—although the specific *commodity* changed over time. In the first years of Portuguese colonization, the commodity was brazilwood. Then, in the 16th and 17th centuries, sugarcane became Brazil's primary source of wealth. Precious metals (gold and silver) and gems (diamonds and emeralds) replaced sugarcane in the 18th century. Finally, in the 19th century, coffee became the country's key export. Meanwhile, agriculture and cattle raising had developed for local markets inside Brazil.

A first surge of industrialization took place during the years of World War I (1914–18), when factories appeared for manufacturing. But it was only from the 1930s onward that Brazil reached a level of modern economic performance. In the 1940s, Brazil's first steel plant was built in the state of Rio de Janeiro, with U.S. financing.

From the 1950s through the 1970s Brazil's industrial base expanded into the automobile industry, petrochemicals, and steel. In the decades after World War II, the annual growth rate of Brazil's economy was among the highest in the world. During the 1970s Brazilian, U.S., European, and Japanese banks invested heavily in Brazil, further fueling the nation's economy.

In the early 1980s, however, a rise in interest rates on loans affected international investors. Brazil, like many other nations, cut back on development because *capital* was not as readily available. The price of goods rose steeply—hitting the poorest Brazilians particularly hard—but government measures to control runaway inflation failed.

Finally, in the early 1990s, Brazil instituted a series of far-reaching economic reforms. Some of these, for instance, put state monopolies in steel, telecommunications, and electricity into private hands; promoted foreign investment; and opened more opportunities for trade.

In 1994, after several unsuccessful attempts to bring down inflation, the Brazilian government introduced the *Plano Real* (Real Plan), which kept a tight rein on Brazil's money supply and tied its currency to the approximate worth of the U.S. dollar. The plan worked: prices stabilized, inflation dropped, and foreign investment returned to Brazil.

By the end of the decade, however, Brazil was forced to stop pegging the real—which was deemed overvalued—to the dollar. After the decision to allow the currency to float freely, the real plummeted.

Poor Brazilians protest landlessness. Much of the land in Brazil is controlled by a small group of wealthy people.

Agriculture and Forest Products

Agriculture, which employs about 20 percent of Brazil's labor force, accounts for 5.5 percent of the country's gross domestic product and generates about one-third of its export earnings. Brazil is the world's largest coffee producer, and one of the largest producers of sugar and soybeans. Brazil is also one of the world's largest producers of oranges, bananas, and papaws, a small tropical fruit. Ranching is important as well: there are 172 million head of cattle in Brazil.

Brazil's abundant forests provide valuable resources, though deforestation—particularly in the Amazon rain forest—has long been a concern of environmentalists. Timber is a major export. About 40 percent of Brazil's timber comes from the northeastern part of the country, particularly the state of Bahia; plantations in the south and southeast account for another 20 percent of the total. Tropical hardwoods such as mahogany, used in making fine furniture, are another valuable commodity.

Industry

Overall, about 14 percent of Brazil's labor force works in industry, with the employment leaders being food and metal processing, automobiles, chemicals, and textiles. In terms of sales, the top industries are chemicals, foodstuffs, metals, vehicles, and engineering. Industry accounts for nearly 30 percent of Brazil's GDP.

The mining industry, which supplies Brazil with a vital source of industrial raw materials at home, also provides 10.2 percent of the nation's

Quick Facts: The Economy of Brazil

Gross domestic product (GDP*):
$1.836 trillion (purchasing power parity)

GDP per capita: $9,700

Inflation: 3.6%

Natural resources: bauxite, gold, iron ore, manganese, nickel, phosphates, platinum, tin, uranium, petroleum, hydropower, timber

Agriculture (5.5% of GDP): coffee, soybeans, wheat, rice, corn, sugarcane, cocoa, citrus, beef (2000 est.)

Industry (28.7% of GDP): textiles, shoes, chemicals, cement, lumber, iron ore, tin, steel, aircraft, motor vehicles and parts, other machinery and equipment (2000 est.)

Services (65.8% of GDP): banks, transportation and communication companies; schools, hospitals, and government agencies; tourism (2000 est.)

Foreign trade:

Exports—$160.6 billion: transport equipment, iron ore, soybeans, footwear, coffee, autos

Imports—$120.6 billion: machinery, electrical and transport equipment, chemical products, oil, automotive parts, electronics

Currency exchange rate: 1.63 reals = US $1 (August 2008).

* GDP = total value of goods and services produced annually.
All figures are 2007 estimates unless otherwise noted.

Sources: CIA World Factbook 2008; Bloomberg.com

export earnings. Brazil is one of the world's largest exporters of iron ore, and an important source of gold, tin, and manganese. Bauxite, nickel, zinc, copper, and the metallic element molybdenum are also mined. Overall, Brazil produces 90 percent of the world's supply of gems, including diamonds, topazes, and emeralds.

Oil was first discovered in northeastern Brazil in 1939. Offshore oil fields account for about 85 percent of production and contain about 80 percent of

Brazil's known reserves—10.3 billion barrels. New oil fields were discovered in Rio de Janeiro—the nation's largest oil producer—and off the shore of Sergipe in 1996. Significant oil and natural gas fields have also been found in the Amazon region.

The manufacturing sector has been a key to Brazil's economic development, enjoying periods of rapid growth, especially in the late 1950s and the 1970s. Brazil has become a leading producer of steel. Automobiles, aircraft, electrical goods, and chemicals are other important industrial products.

Services

In terms of percentage of labor force employed and percentage of GDP, services make up the largest sector of Brazil's economy. A majority (66 percent) of the labor force works in the service sector, which accounts for over 60

Traders work on the floor of the Brazilian Stock Exchange, the largest financial market in Latin America.

percent of the country's GDP. Among the service sector's important fields are banking, transportation, health care, education, and communications.

With its beaches, wildlife, and cities such as Rio de Janeiro, Brazil is a popular destination for tourists. Many of Brazil's service-sector jobs support tourism.

One category of service-sector employment deserves particular mention, and not necessarily in a positive light: government. Brazil has long been known for its bloated bureaucracy (unelected government officials), and citizens frequently complain about the amount of paperwork, time, and inconvenience involved in even routine official dealings such as obtaining a driver's license, birth certificate, or business license. (Bribing the responsible government workers, Brazilians know, can make things much easier.) In the late 1990s, before President Cardoso instituted a program to shrink the bureaucracy, there were more than 1,770 categories of public-service jobs, and the federal workforce exceeded 1.3 million employees.

Continuing Challenges

The government faces increasing pressure to fix what is perhaps the world's most unfair distribution of wealth. At the end of the 20th century, the richest 20 percent of the population received 63 percent of the nation's income, while an estimated 28.7 percent were living on less than $1 a day. Two-thirds of the country's farmable land is owned by as few as 3 percent of its people. In addition, social conditions are harsh in the big cities of Rio de Janeiro and São Paulo, where there are tens of thousands of street children and where a third of the population lives in *favelas*, or slums.

(Opposite) A woman participates in a Carnival parade in Rio de Janeiro. Carnival, celebrated just before the start of the Christian season of Lent, is Brazil's most famous festival. (Right) A soccer star celebrates Brazil's victory over the German team in the 2002 World Cup final. Soccer (*futebol*) is a passion for many Brazilians.

4 A Stew of Peoples and Cultures

BRAZIL'S POPULATION IS very diverse. This diversity is the result of intermingling between Amerindians, Portuguese settlers, and African slaves. Likewise, Brazilian culture has been shaped not only by the Portuguese—who gave the country its principal common religion and language—but also by Indians, descendants of African slaves, and settlers from Europe, the Middle East, and Asia.

Brazil is the only Latin American country settled by the Portuguese. Before the Portuguese arrived in 1500, many Amerindian tribes sparsely populated the land. In the mid-16th century the Portuguese began to import African slaves to work in mines and on plantations. The ethnic mix among these three groups, along with other European peoples who immigrated to

Quick Facts: The People of Brazil

Population: 191, 908, 598

Ethnic groups: white 53.7%, mulatto (mixed white and black) 38.5%, black 6.2%, other (includes Japanese, Arab, Amerindian) 0.9%, unspecified 0.7%

Age structure:
0–4 years: 24.9%
15–64 years: 68.7%
65 years and over: 6.4%

Population growth rate: 0.98%

Birth rate: 16.04 births/1,000 population

Death rate: 6.22 deaths/1,000 population

Infant mortality rate: 26.67 deaths/1,000 live births

Life expectancy at birth:
total population: 72.51 years
male: 68.57 years
female: 76.64 years

Total fertility rate: 1.86 children born/woman

Religions: Roman Catholic 73.6%, Protestant 15.4%, Spiritualist 1.3%, Bantu/voodoo 0.3%, other 1.8%, unspecified 0.2%, none 7.4% (2000 est.)

Languages: Portuguese (official), Spanish, English, French

Literacy (age 15 and older): 88.6% (2006 est.)

All figures are 2008 estimates unless otherwise noted. Source: CIA World Factbook 2008.

Brazil after 1850, has contributed to some distinctly Brazilian cultural forms, especially in music and architecture. Distinct cultures also continue to survive among Afro-Brazilians, non-Portuguese immigrants from Europe and Asia, and isolated pockets of Indians. Portuguese is spoken by all Brazilians, but the language has absorbed hundreds of words from Indian and African languages. Accents, dialects, and slang vary by region.

Variety in All Walks of Life

Brazil is officially a Catholic country, but in practice the country's religious life also includes Indian *animism*, African cults, Afro-Catholic *syncretism*, and Kardecism, a spiritualist religion embracing Eastern mysticism, which is gaining popularity with white Brazilians.

Architecture was the first art form in Brazil that developed into a distinctively Brazilian style, through the blending of European and African influences. During the 18th century, wealth created by sugar plantations and gold mines went into the building of gorgeous churches and public buildings in the regions of Bahia, Pernambuco, and Minas Gerais. After independence in 1822, Brazilian architects turned away from their Portuguese inheritance and took inspiration from other sources.

Brazilian colonial literature was based on Old World models, steeped in *classical* and Roman Catholic traditions. After independence, writers worked to create a uniquely Brazilian literary style. The late 19th century produced one of Brazil's most important literary figures: Joaquim Maria

Tradition meets technology: members of an indigenous Brazilian tribe, the Truka, use a public telephone inside a courthouse in Brasília.

Machado de Assis, whose works include *Quincas borba* (1891; translated in 1954 as *Philosopher or Dog?*) and *Dom Casmurro* (1899; translated 1953). Many of his books examine the joys and sorrows of being human and contain a rather pessimistic strain. In the early 20th century, writers tended to describe the experiences of immigrants. In recent years, Brazilian writers have explored the question of what it means to be Brazilian in terms of culture and society.

Brazilian music has always been characterized by great diversity and shaped by musical influences from three continents. It is still developing new and original forms. The samba, which reached its height of popularity in the 1930s, is a mixture of Spanish bolero with the cadences and rhythms of African music. In the 1960s, a bossa nova craze from Brazil swept the United States, characterized by songs such as "The Girl from Ipanema"—although the sound was influenced by North American jazz. More recently, the lambada, influenced by Caribbean rhythms, became internationally popular in the 1980s.

Brazilian Cuisine

When the Portuguese arrived in South America, the foodstuffs of the native tribes were simple. As the Portuguese and Indian cultures blended, however, so did the cuisine. Locally gathered cassava, fruit, chilies, game, and fish combined with imported olive oil, dried cod, stews, and numerous desserts. African slaves introduced palm oil, coconuts, dried shrimp, and other typical African foods.

Today, every region has its own festive dishes drawn from the past, but *feijoada* (bean stew), which originated in Rio de Janeiro, is widely considered the most typical of Brazilian dishes. It is often served to visitors, who enjoy the pot of black beans in thick sauce, cooked with an abundance of fresh meat. The beans are usually served separately on one dish and the meat on another, accompanied by finely sliced kale (quick-fried with a little oil and garlic), cassava flour or *farofa* (flour mixed with butter), and slices of fresh orange.

In people's homes, large meals feature various dishes served together, except for soup (which comes at the beginning) and dessert (at the end). The dishes usually include plain rice; black beans or kidney beans in thick sauce; meat, poultry, or fish; a green salad; cooked vegetables; and a little fried cake. As side dishes there will be sausage with cassava flour or a *farofa*. Pickled chilies or chili sauce add spice to a meal. Brazilians enjoy the kind of food that can be eaten with their hands in small bites.

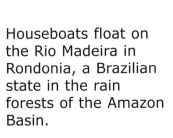

Houseboats float on the Rio Madeira in Rondonia, a Brazilian state in the rain forests of the Amazon Basin.

(Opposite) The statue of Christ the Redeemer, one of Brazil's most famous landmarks, looms over Rio de Janeiro atop Corcovado Mountain. The statue is 125 feet (38 meters) tall. (Right) The skyline of São Paulo, Brazil's largest city, which is home to more than 10 million people.

5 Brazil's Colorful, Crowded Cities

UNTIL THE MID-1960s more Brazilians lived in the countryside than in towns. But since then, the lure of jobs has drawn workers to the larger cities, swelling them in size. Today, more than 80 percent of Brazil's people live in urban areas, and one-third live in cities having more than 1 million inhabitants. Many of Brazil's larger cities have extensive slums whose residents lack access to clean water, electricity, and health care, compounding the problems of poverty, hunger, and disease. Homelessness—especially among children and young teens—is also a major social problem, particularly in São Paulo and Rio de Janeiro.

Brazil has enjoyed some success in combating another social problem that is most prevalent in cities: *AIDS*. A disease caused by a virus called HIV, AIDS attacks the immune system. Brazil's program to combat the spread of AIDS has become a model for other developing countries. Through education and health care, Brazil has succeeded in stabilizing the rate of HIV infection (estimated at 0.57 percent in 1999) and reducing the number of AIDS-related deaths (estimated at 18,000 in 1999).

The Pressures of Population

In Brazil, the population density varies greatly by region. The most densely peopled states are Rio de Janeiro, the Federal District, and São Paulo. The least populous state is the interior region of Amazonas. About 80 percent of Brazil's population lives within 220 miles (354 km) of the coast.

If overcrowding in the big cities has strained the government's ability to provide basic services to all citizens, in villages and towns government resources are stretched even thinner. Little development has taken place in the countryside. For example, 95 percent of urban dwellers have access to safe drinking water, but only 53 percent do in the countryside. Most of the available work is only for laborers, and wages are lower than in the cities. A family wage earner in the rural northeastern part of the country earns about half as much as a city worker in the southeastern part. He is also twice as likely to be *illiterate*, and his life expectancy is 10 years lower. A key challenge facing the government is removing the inequality of opportunities for Brazilians.

Profiles of the Major Cities

The largest city in Brazil is São Paulo, the main industrial center of the nation. São Paulo is also the largest city in South America. The former capital of Brazil, Rio de Janeiro, ranks second. It is an important port and commercial center. Other important cities include Salvador, the capital of Bahia; Belo Horizonte, a major industrial and commercial city in Minas Gerais; and Brasília, the national capital of Brazil. Each of these cities forms the core of a larger urban area. There are six other cities in Brazil with more than a million inhabitants: Manaus, a port on the Río Negro near its *confluence* with the Amazon; Belém, a northern port near the mouth of the Amazon; Fortaleza and Recife, along the northeastern coast; and Curitiba and Pôrto Alegre in the south.

The Nossa Senhora da Sé Cathedral in Rio Branco. Brazil has many beautiful cathedrals and churches; four-fifths of the population is Roman Catholic.

São Paulo

São Paulo sits on a plateau 2,493 feet (760 meters) above sea level and 45 miles (72 km) from the coast. Founded in 1554 by the Jesuits, its original purpose was to serve as a mission center for early settlers and Indians. For a long time it remained a small town. Around 1850, however, it began to grow, fueled by the highly productive coffee plantations in the state. By the early 1900s, São Paulo's coffee exports and increasing population provided investment money and manpower, turning the little town into an industrial city. Today the city and its surrounding area are home to more than 20,000 industrial plants of all types and sizes. São Paulo has also evolved into a major financial center to serve the needs of business.

Rio de Janeiro

In 1502 Portuguese explorers arrived at Guanabara Bay, the site of Rio de Janeiro. But it was the French who, in 1555, first established a settlement facing the bay. Twelve years later the Portuguese expelled the French colonists. For almost 150 years, Rio de Janeiro existed as a small Portuguese colony, whose members made a living by farming, fishing, and exporting brazilwood and sugarcane. The building of a road in 1704 from Rio to the gold mines of Minas Gerais transformed the town into a major center of transportation, commerce, and wealth. The French captured Rio in 1710 and forced the Portuguese to pay ransom for its return.

When the government of Brazil moved from Salvador to Rio de Janeiro in 1763, the city became one of the major capitals of South America. In 1808

Brazil's 10 Largest Cities

	Population			Population
1. **São Paulo**	10,057,700	6. **Brasília**		1,954,400
2. **Rio de Janeiro**	6,029,300	7. **Curitiba**		1,642,300
3. **Salvador**	2,539,500	8. **Manaus**		1,524,600
4. **Belo Horizonte**	2,307,800	9. **Recife**		1,464,100
5. **Fortaleza**	2,230,800	10. **Pôrto Alegre**		1,355,100

Figures are 2002 estimates.

Portugal's exiled royal family chose Rio as their refuge from Napoleon's armies. Rio grew further in size and took on a European flavor. In 1822 it became the capital of the independent Brazilian Empire. With the overthrow of the Portuguese monarchy in 1889, Rio became the capital of the Brazilian republic. By 1900 Rio's population had grown to about 800,000, fueled by the success of coffee growing. After World War II, Rio prospered from increasing commerce and international trade.

But since the second half of the 18th century, Brazil's government had been weighing whether to transfer the seat of government from Rio de Janeiro to some inland area, safe from naval attacks. In 1960 the capital of the nation was transferred to Brasília. This marked a dramatic change for Rio, resulting in a loss of political status and prestige. In any event, this second-largest city in Brazil is still a major cultural capital. Rio de Janeiro has a majestic beauty, with a magnificent bay, dazzling beaches, and an abruptly rising mountain range covered by a luxuriant tropical forest.

Many poor people in Brazil's large cities live in *favelas*, or slums, such as this one in Rio de Janeiro.

Combined with a mild climate, Rio's landscape makes it one of the most beautiful cities in the world, justifying its title of "Marvelous City" (*Cidade Maravilhosa*).

Brasília

In 1956 construction began on the new capital. Brasília is located in the 2,245-square-mile (5,812-sq-km) Federal District, on an otherwise sparsely inhabited plateau carved out of the state of Goiás. It sits 746 miles (1,201 km) from the former capital of Rio de Janeiro. Brazilian architect and urban planner Lúcio Costa won the competition held for designing Brasília's complete layout. Oscar Niemeyer, a Brazilian architect, designed the major government buildings. Landscape designer Roberto Burle Marx planned the landscaping and selected the vegetation to add a vivid green backdrop to the otherwise dry, yellow landscape of the *savanna*. On April 21, 1960, Brasília was officially inaugurated and started functioning as the new capital of Brazil.

Salvador

Salvador, capital of the state of Bahia, was the first major port and the capital of colonial Brazil for almost two centuries. The city lies between green tropical hills and broad beaches along the Bay of Todos os Santos. It was built on two levels: administration buildings and residences on the hills; forts, docks, and warehouses on the beaches. Salvador is still divided into upper and lower cities.

From 1500 to 1815 Salvador was the nation's busiest port. Prized shipments of sugar from the northeast and gold and diamonds from the mines in the south passed through Salvador. It was a golden age for the city. Many of the city's *baroque* churches, private homes, squares, and even the hand-chipped paving bricks have been preserved as part of Brazil's historic past.

In Salvador, the African influence on Brazilian culture remains prominent. Spicy dishes are still called by their African names (*caruru, vatapá, acarajé*). *Candomblé* ceremonies honor both African deities and Catholic holidays. *Capoeira* schools teach an African form of ritualistic fighting.

Belo Horizonte

Belo Horizonte, founded in 1897, was the first modern planned Brazilian city. It was designed specially to serve as the capital of the state of Minas Gerais. Its wide, landscaped avenues and carefully laid-out residential suburbs have been cramped by a high rate of urban development over the last 30 years, though.

Belo Horizonte is the distribution and processing center of a rich agricultural, mining, and industrial complex. Its chief manufactured items are steel, steel products, automobiles, and textiles. Factories process gold, manganese, and gemstones from the surrounding region. Belo Horizonte is also a leading cultural center, boasting three universities, a historical museum, numerous libraries, and several sports stadiums. The climate is refreshing and cool.

Curitiba

Curitiba, standing some 3,000 feet (915 meters) above sea level on the plateau of Serra do Mar, is the capital of the state of Paraná. Since the late 1800s, Curitiba's bracing climate and lovely location have attracted immigrants of Slav, German, and Italian origin. Curitiba grew rapidly after 1950, becoming a major city yet keeping its comfortable lifestyle. The city's prosperity stems from its role as a commercial and processing center for the surrounding ranches and huge farms.

Recife

Recife began as a port in 1709. Interestingly, for a time it was under Dutch control and served as a refuge for Jews fleeing the Spanish Inquisition. When the Portuguese conquered the city, its Jewish residents left or practiced in secret. The capital of the northeastern state of Pernambuco, Recife is a fast-growing urban area that has been called the "Venice of Brazil" because it is cut through by numerous waterways and connected by many bridges. Local fishermen go out onto the high seas in *jangadas*, crude log rafts with beautiful sails unique to the area that require expert navigational skills to maneuver. Recife exports great quantities sugar, cotton, and coffee.

Pôrto Alegre

Pôrto Alegre, the largest city in the south of Brazil, is the capital of the state of Rio Grande do Sul. Immigrants from the Azores, a group of Portuguese-owned islands in the Atlantic Ocean, founded the city in 1742. Since the 19th century the city has received numerous German and Italian immigrants. Lying as it does at the junction of five rivers, it has become an important port, as well as one of Brazil's chief industrial and commercial centers. Pôrto Alegre exports products from the surrounding agricultural region, including leather, canned beef, and rice.

An estimated 2.5 million people packed the beaches of Rio de Janeiro to watch a spectacular New Year's fireworks display, January 1, 2000.

A Calendar of Brazilian Festivals

Brazil is known for its colorful festivals and holidays, many of which feature parades, costumes, music, and especially dancing. Like other aspects of its culture, Brazil's festivals mix elements of Amerindian, Portuguese, and African traditions and customs.

January

Brazilians celebrate **New Year's** with fireworks that start at midnight. Also at the stroke of midnight, residents of Rio de Janeiro dash through the streets to the beach. There they light candles on the sand or throw flowers into the ocean, offerings to the sea goddess. For good luck in the year to come, many Brazilians also wear white clothing or wade into the water and jump seven waves.

January 6 is the Catholic holiday of **Epiphany**, which commemorates the visit of the Three Kings to the baby Jesus.

February

Carnival, Brazil's most famous festival, is celebrated on the four days before Ash Wednesday, the beginning of the Christian season of Lent. It may fall in February or March. Various cities, including Salvador and Recife, hold major Carnival celebrations, but by far the biggest and most famous is Rio de Janeiro's. Highlights of Carnival include the Samba Parade, during which samba "schools" (large, often community-based clubs) compete against one another. Each samba school may have up to 5,000 elaborately costumed members and six to eight floats. It may take one school more than an hour to dance and parade past the judges and the thousands of paying spectators. Helicopters hovering overhead capture the spectacle for a nationwide television audience. Much less elaborate but, Brazilians say, equally fun is the Street Carnival—basically a series of moving parties everyone is welcome to join.

March

Like Christians the world over, Brazilians celebrate **Easter**, which commemorates the resurrection of Jesus. Easter may fall either in March or in April.

June

Festas Juninas, midwinter festival days honoring the saints, are important occasions in Catholic Brazil. Three of the country's favorite saints are celebrated: St. Anthony (June 13), St. John (June 24), and St. Peter (June 29). Parati's baroque churches, colorful fishing wharfs, and Old World atmosphere are particularly alive during the festivities.

Also in June, cattle-raising areas celebrate the religious story of a slave who kills his master's ox and must resurrect it or be put to death himself. In addition to dancing and street processions, the folk tale is reenacted by costumed dancers.

August

The Festival of the Goddess of the Sea (Iemanjá), celebrated on New Year's in Rio, is celebrated June 15 on Futuro Beach in the

A Calendar of Brazilian Festivals

city of Fortaleza. People begin arriving on the beach at noon from more than 150 nearby churches, and each congregation stakes out a particular piece of beach. By late afternoon the celebration is in full swing, with church members beating drums and chanting in their white-and-blue robes, or parading images of Iemanjá up and down the beach.

September

On the 7th of the month, Brazil marks **Independence Day**. On that date in 1822, Pedro I proclaimed Brazil's independence from Portugal.

October

October 12, the feast day of Brazil's patron saint, **Nossa Senhora da Aparecida** (Our Lady of Aparecida) is also the climax of the Amazon region's largest annual festival. Held in Belém, it features a large procession in which crowds battle for the right to carry the "miracle car" holding the image of the Virgin. The church is decked out with lights, and bands play music nonstop.

November

On **All Souls' Day** (November 2), Brazilians remember and pray for the souls of the departed.

November 15 is **Proclamation Day**. It celebrates the proclaiming of the Brazilian republic in 1889.

December

On December 25, Brazilians, like Christians everywhere, celebrate **Christmas.**

On the 29th, the **Festival of Jesus of Navigators**, held in Salvador and Aracaju, begins (it ends on January 1). The festival, which includes four days of music, dancing, feasting, and drinking, also features hundreds of small, wildly festooned boats off the beach in Salvador and on the Sergipe River in Aracaju.

Recipes

Sopa de Palmito (**Cream of Palm Heart Soup**)

(Serves 4)
1 can hearts of palm
4 tbsp butter
4 tbsp flour
2 cups vegetable stock
1 cup milk
1 cup heavy cream
White pepper, to taste

Directions:
1. Drain and rinse the palm hearts. Place in a food processor and puree.
2. Melt butter in a sauté pan. Add flour and cook over low heat, stirring constantly, creating a thick, creamy sauce.
3. Slowly add warm vegetable stock, stirring with a wire whip so it is lump free. Blend in the palm hearts. Add the milk and cream just before serving.
4. Bring to serving temperature, but do not allow to boil. Add a little pepper to accent the taste.

Arroz Brasileiro (**Brazilian-Style Rice**)

(Serves 12)
4 cups long-grain rice
8 cups water
1 medium onion, chopped
3 tbsp olive oil
Salt to taste

Directions:
1. Heat the olive oil in a large saucepan over medium heat.
2. Add the chopped onion and cook until limp. Do not let it brown!
3. Add the rice and sauté until the grains become shiny. Add the water, cover the pan, and cook over low heat until all the water is absorbed and the grains are tender.

Fruit Punch *Batida*

(Serves 4)
2 cups of different fruit juices
1/2 cup of sweetened condensed milk
1 can ginger ale
1/2 cup ice cubes

Directions:
1. Combine all ingredients except ice cubes in a blender and mix.
2. Add ice cubes while blender is running and continue mixing until ice is crushed.
3. Serve immediately.

Brazilian Black Bean *Feijoada*

(Serves 8)
2 tbsp olive oil
1 cup chopped onions
1 tbsp grated ginger
1/4 tsp black or cayenne pepper
1/2 tsp ground cumin
2 cans black beans (15 oz. each)
2 tbsp apple cider vinegar
1 tsp salt
6 cups spicy tomato juice

Directions:
1. Heat oil, then sauté onions until clear.
2. Add remaining ingredients and simmer for 30 minutes.

Creme de Abacate **(Avocado Cream)**

(Serves 4)
2 medium avocados
2 tbsp lime juice
4 tbsp granulated sugar
1/4 cup ice water

Directions:
1. Peel and slice the avocado, discarding the seed.
2. Place fruit, lime juice, and sugar in a food processor or blender.
3. Puree at high speed until completely smooth.
4. Add a little water if the puree is very stiff (some prefer white grape juice). It should be absolutely smooth and creamy. Serve in a clear glass.

Pastel Frito **(Deep-fried Filled Pastry)**

(Serves 20)
2 cups all-purpose flour
1 tbsp almond flavoring
1 tbsp margarine
1/3 cup warm water with 2 pinches of salt
1/2 tsp baking powder
1 egg
4 cups vegetable oil for deep-frying

Directions:
1. Sift the flour with baking powder.
2. In a large bowl, mix in the sifted flour, margarine, almond flavoring, and egg. Mix well while adding the warm water until mixture turns doughy. (Or you can prepare the dough in an electric mixer.)
3. Move the dough to a flat surface and knead it for 15 minutes. Use a rolling pin to flatten the dough.
4. Fold the dough over a couple times and flatten it again until you get a big, thin pancake.
5. Sprinkle the surface lightly with sugar.
6. Use a glass or a cookie cutter to cut circles of dough. Place a dab of jelly, jam, a piece of banana, date, or filling in the middle of each. Fold the circle of dough shut, pinching the seam with your fingers.
7. Deep-fry the pastry in vegetable oil at 350°F until golden brown.
8. Pat dry in a paper towel and let cool.

Glossary

abolitionist—one who advocates the ending of slavery.

AIDS—a serious, often fatal disease of the immune system that is caused by the virus HIV.

animism—the worship of animal and nature spirits.

baroque—an artistic style that flourished from the 16th to the mid-18th century and that was characterized by complexity, extravagance, and bold ornamentation.

capital—investment money.

classical—relating to the ancient Greeks or Romans, especially with regard to their art, architecture, and literature.

coastal plain—flat land adjacent to a coast.

commodity—any economic good, such as an agricultural or mining product.

confluence—the place where rivers or streams come together.

coup—the sudden overthrow of a government by a small group using violence or the threat of violence.

elite—a group enjoying privileged or superior status.

fauna—an area's animal life.

flora—an area's plant life.

gross domestic product (GDP)—the total value of all the goods and services produced by a nation in a one-year period.

illiterate—unable to read or write.

indigenous—native or original to a particular place.

inflation—a steady increase in consumer prices.

Glossary

mulatto—a person of mixed white and black ancestry.

plateau—an elevated, level expanse of land.

republic—a government in which a body of citizens entitled to vote elects representatives to exercise power under the law.

revenue—income derived from sales.

savanna—low-lying grasslands.

syncretism—a combination of different systems of belief.

trade winds—prevailing winds of the Tropics that blow toward the equator.

tributaries—rivers and streams that feed larger bodies of water.

Project and Report Ideas

Investigate Brazil's wildlife

Introduce your classmates to some of the strange and fascinating animals that can be found in Brazil. Describe their appearance, eating habits, and behavior. Find or draw pictures.

Flag poster

Make your own flag representing Brazil. Pick a piece of colored construction paper as your background. Then try to think of at least three things that represent Brazil, and paste them into the middle of your flag. You can create those out of construction paper, cut them out of a magazine, or print them off the Internet. Next, find a picture of the real flag of Brazil. Create a copy of that flag using construction paper and other materials. Paste both finished flags onto a large piece of white poster board so you can compare them. Leave space for a page beneath the flags. Then write a page explaining why you chose the shapes for your flag and what the differences are between your flag and the real one. Try to find out the history behind the flag of Brazil and include that in your report. Paste your finished report on the poster board underneath the two flags. Hang the finished poster on a wall in your classroom for everyone to see.

Short reports

In one-page reports, answer these questions:
- What makes an area a rain forest?
- Where was the Portuguese Empire and when did it exist?
- What do the precious stones that come from Brazil look like?
- Who were the Jesuit priests?
- How did Brasília become the capital of Brazil?

Project and Report Ideas

Brazilian bios

Write a one-page biography on any of the following:
- Vasco da Gama
- Pedro Álvares Cabral
- Pedro I, emperor of Brazil
- Getúlio Vargas
- Joaquim Maria Machado de Assis

Maps, charts, and graphs

- Create a bar graph showing the populations of Brazil's 10 largest cities.
- Show with three drawings how the area of the Amazon rain forest has changed over the last 50 years.
- Population map: using different colors, show how Brazil's population is clustered around the largest cities.

Chronology

1499	Portuguese explorer Vasco da Gama returns to Portugal, having completed the first successful sea voyage from western Europe around the tip of Africa to India and back.
1500	On April 22, Pedro Álvares Cabral, sailing from Portugal to the East Indies, lands on the eastern coast of South America (what is now Brazil); he claims the land for Portugal.
1531	King João III of Portugal sends the first settlers to Brazil.
1549	Jesuit priests arrive in Brazil; eventually they will provide some protection for the indigenous people.
1690s	Gold is discovered in Minas Gerais.
1763	Brazil's colonial capital is moved from Salvador to Rio de Janeiro.
1822	Pedro, the son of King João VI, declares Brazil's independence from Portugal and crowns himself Pedro I, emperor of Brazil.
1831	Pedro I abdicates his Brazilian throne as a result of an unsuccessful war with Argentina.
1888	Slavery is abolished in Brazil; over the next decade, a large influx of European immigrants arrives.
1889	The monarchy is overthrown, and a federal republic is established in Brazil with the central government controlled by coffee interests.
1930	A popular uprising places Getúlio Vargas at the head of a revolutionary government; the theme of the government is to reform politics and modernize Brazil.
1954	Vargas commits suicide amid political and economic turbulence.
1956–61	Juscelino Kubitschek is president, helping Brazil achieve rapid economic growth.

1960	Kubitschek moves capital to Brasília.
1964	A military coup ushers in 25 years of non-democratic rule.
1985	Military hands back power to the civilian government.
1989	Fernando Collor de Mello is elected president.
1992	Collor resigns after being accused of corruption; he is replaced by Vice President Itamar Franco.
1994	Fernando Henrique Cardoso is elected president.
1997	Brazil's constitution is changed to allow the president to run for reelection, and Cardoso is elected the following year.
2000	Brazil marks its 500th anniversary, but indigenous Indians protest the celebrations, saying that the country has a history of injustice towards their population.
2001	The Brazilian government announces the end of a development program that critics say had a catastrophic impact on the Amazon.
2002	Leftist former union organizer Luiz Inácio Lula da Silva wins presidential election in a landslide; promises to fight hunger and create jobs through large public-works projects.
2004	In September, hundreds of politicians and government officials are accused of involvement in a major corruption scandal.
2006	Lula da Silva is reelected, despite corruption scandals in his Workers' Party.
2007	A plane crash kills nearly 200 in São Paulo, leading to speculation about the safety of Brazil's infrastructure.
2008	Brazil's Indian protection agency releases photographs of a previously unknown indigenous group living in the Amazon rainforest.

Further Reading/Internet Resources

Deckker, Zilah. *Brazil*. Des Moines: National Geographic Children's Books, 2008.

McCann, Bryan. *Hello, Hello Brazil: Popular Music in the Making of Modern Brazil*. Durham, N.C.: Duke University Press, 2004.

Poelzl, Volker. *Brazil: A Survival Guide to Customs and Etiquette*. Tarrytown, N.Y.: Marshall Cavendish, 2007.

Sheen, Barbara. *Foods of Brazil*. Detroit: KidHaven Press, 2008.

St. Louis, Regis, et al. *Brazil*. Oakland, Calif.: Lonely Planet, 2008.

Travel Information

http://www.lonelyplanet.com/destinations/south_america/brazil/
http://www.globalgourmet.com/destinations/brazil/brazilfest.html
http://www.gringoes.com/
http://www.vivabrazil.com/

History and Geography

http://www.lib.utexas.edu/maps/brazil.html
http://www.geographia.com/brazil/brazihistory.htm
http://www.rain-tree.com/

Economic and Political Information

http://www.state.gov/r/pa/ei/bgn/35640.htm
http://www.brazilcouncil.org/

Ministerio Das Relações Exteriores
Assessoria de Comunicação Social
Palácio Itamaraty - Térreo - Brasilia, DF - 70170-900
(5561) 211-6162/6163
Acs@mre.gov.br

U.S. Department of Commerce
Office of Latin America and the Caribbean
International Trade Administration
14th and Constitution Ave., NW
Washington, DC 20230
(202) 482-0428
1-800-USA-TRADE
http://www.ita.doc.gov

Brazilian Embassy in Washington
3006 Massachusetts Ave., NW
Washington, DC 20008
(202) 238-2700
http://www.brasilemb.org/

Index

Index/Picture Credits

Contributors

Senior Consulting Editor **James D. Henderson** is professor of international studies at Coastal Carolina University. He is the author of *Conservative Thought in Twentieth Century Latin America: The Ideals of Laureano Gómez* (1988; Spanish edition *Las ideas de Laureano Gómez* published in 1985); *When Colombia Bled: A History of the Violence in Tolima* (1985; Spanish edition *Cuando Colombia se desangró, una historia de la Violencia en metrópoli y provincia*, 1984); and coauthor of *A Reference Guide to Latin American History* (2000) and *Ten Notable Women of Latin America* (1978).

Mr. Henderson earned a bachelor's degree in history from Centenary College of Louisiana, and a master's degree in history from the University of Arizona. He then spent three years in the Peace Corps, serving in Colombia, before earning his doctorate in Latin American history in 1972 at Texas Christian University.

Charles J. Shields is the author of 20 books for young people. He has degrees in English and history from the University of Illinois, Urbana-Champaign. Before turning to writing full time, he was chairman of the English and guidance departments at Homewood-Flossmoor High School in Flossmoor, Illinois. He lives in Homewood, a suburb of Chicago, with his wife, Guadalupe, a former elementary school principal and now an educational consultant to the Chicago Public Schools.